D1608267

NYC Color Guide to Freight and Passenger Equipment

by
David R. Sweetland and Robert J. Yanosey

Published by
Morning Sun Books, Inc.
11 Sussex Court
Edison, N.J. 08820
Library of Congress Catalog Card Number: 93-080950
Layout by R. J. Yanosey of Morning Sun Books.

First Printing
ISBN 1-878887-30-0

Dedication

For Emery Gulash

Acknowledgements

The authors wish to express their sincere thanks to the many photographers who contributed their efforts to this work. They are in alphabetical order: Craig Bossler, Michael Bradley, H.E. Brouse, Mike Bullock, Bill Clynes, David Conner, George Ford, Emery Gulash, Bob Hart, William Herrmann, Al Holtz, Dick Kuelbs, Emmons Lancaster, Dave McKay, Arthur Mitchell, Ed Nowak, Dick Short, Dwight Smith, Ed Stoll, J.W. Swanberg, Roy Ward, and Dennis Wood. Art Peterson lent us a photo from his collection, Mitch Dakelman several from the NRHS Echternacht collection, and one was used courtesy of *Collectables from Bob's Photos*. Gentlemen, you are to be commended for having the wisdom to photograph equipment while everyone else was focusing on locomotives and trains.

Index

NYC Color Guide to Freight and Passenger Equipment

In the year 1826, John Quincy Adams was the nation's sixth president and the roots of the New York Central System began to take hold as the New York State legislature authorized creation of the "Mohawk and Hudson RR Company." Five years later the wood-burning *De Witt Clinton* chuffed up Albany hill with three coaches of dignitaries. From those three "stage coaches on rails" sprang the likes of the TWENTIETH CENTURY LIMITED, the EMPIRE STATE EXPRESS and some of the most celebrated trains in the world. This *Color Guide* to freight and passenger equipment will attempt to chronicle the rolling stock of the great New York Central System, giving the reader a diverse sampling of the road's equipment during the years when color film was in use.

If one was to pick up a New York Central Annual Report from the year 1950, he would get a good impression of what the road was thinking - equipment wise - during the post World War II modernization years. In this report, the road was justifiably proud of its passenger service and boasted of its new twin-unit passenger car washer at Mott Haven and even the addition of eighty-two "commutation" cars. The report was flush with photos and tales of the "new Toledo passenger terminal" and even the visit of the Dionne quintuplets on a Central passenger train. In total the road spent over $10 million on new passenger cars in this year and looked forward to a revival in this area when all the new equipment was in service.

While the Central still reverently held its passenger service in the highest regard, it certainly could not ignore freight service in 1950. Here the road was spending over a $100 million to replace outmoded equipment left over from the Depression and the toils of the recent world conflict. War (the Korean kind) was still on the mind of the railroad though, and photos of flats hauling Army tanks and box cars right out of Despatch Shops "for expanded defense capacity" were highlighted. The road acquired 6,587 new freight cars by year's end and had another 14,000 on order. There was no elaboration on the types of cars since they were largely typical workhorse 40' box cars, 50-ton hoppers, and other non-specialized flats and gons. The

singular bragging point in the freight line was the expansion of the "expedited *Pacemaker* freight service" that employed "specially equipped cars at passenger train speeds." This coordinated highway truck-high speed box car service was being expanded into the Big Four district.

Jump forward now sixteen years to the 1966 Central Annual Report and the reader receives quite a different impression of the *Water Level Route's* latest equipment. Now the road was losing $16 million a year with its passenger service. Putting a positive spin on this though, the road spoke of a downsizing plan of less than 200-mile shuttle trains *(Empire Service)* and the Cleveland Technical Center's testing of a jet-powered RDC. The Central also pointed out that it had spent $1.6 million to refurbish forty surplus long haul coaches for the New York suburban zone. It was readily apparent to all, however, that the road was desirous of exiting this business wherever it could.

Obviously freight was the apple of Central's eye, and here the road had much to brag about in its 1966 Annual Report. Its innovations and experiments were on the "cutting edge" of American rail freight development. For example, in 1966, the Central was expanding its self-developed *Flexi-Van* container-on-flat system into new terminals. Piggyback was also beginning at Albany, Boston, and other locales and the report spoke of new "Agri-Marketing" efforts aimed at moving grain in high cube covered hoppers instead of 40' box cars. *Flexi-Flo* cement shipments via the road's specialized cars were a true success story and NYC noted how its multi-level rack cars carried over one million new autos and trucks, "nearly 11% of the nation's total production."

Between 1950 and 1966, the Central astutely revamped the transportation product it sold to American industry and the traveling public. The transformation enabled the road to survive during these troubled times of railroading. The key to this survival, after the dedicated Central employees, was the distinct NYC equipment fielded by this company. It is this roster which we will sample within these 128 pages.

Head End

▲ NYC 7957 a 60' baggage car in Pullman green was photographed in Dallas, Texas on December 22, 1961. Built by Barney & Smith in 1914, its old number was NYC 2979. With one 8' and one 6' side door with 4 wheeled trucks, the car was Class F-5 and a member of Lot 826.

(Dick Kuelbs)

▼ Built by ACF in 1921 NYC 8850 also was photographed at Dallas Union Terminal three days later on 12-25-61. The 60' Baggage car was former B&A 897. With truck class R (4-wheel), it was part of Lot 911. *(Dick Kuelbs)*

NYC 7469 was part of Lot 959 and lensed at Fort Worth, Texas on Christmas Day, 1963. Built by ACF in 1924 as NYC 3356, it later became NYC 8396 with truck class Rx.
(Dick Kuelbs)

The NYC had several subsidiaries whose equipment could be identified through markings of "New York Central System" and reporting marks of the subsidiary. P&E (Peoria and Eastern) #912 was a 60' Baggage car from Lot 2115. Photographed at Dallas on New Year's Day 1964, it had a 8' door, and 6' door on each side. With truck class Rx, it still carried the same number it was built as (P&E 912). *(Dick Kuelbs)*

NYC 8420 another 60' baggage part of Lot 960 is seen at Dallas Union Terminal on Oct. 11, 1964. Built by ACF in 1925 as MCRR 1240, it had a 8' door, and 6' door. *(Dick Kuelbs)*

Sixty foot baggage NYC 8447 from Lot 983 was at Palestine, Tex. on the Missouri Pacific on 12-26-61. With 8' and 6' doors, it was originally Big Four 221 when built by ACF in 1925. Truck class T-1x rolled underneath.

(Dick Kuelbs)

NYC 7483 was another 60' baggage from Lot 2068. In Dallas on September 29, 1967, it was built some forty years earlier by ACF in 1927. Originally NYC 3063, then NYC 8536, it had truck class Rx. *(Dick Kuelbs)*

NYC 8696 was a 70' Baggage car from Lot 2108 at Dallas (UT) on January 26, 1963. Cars 8690-8709 were built by ACF in 1929 with 8' and 6' side doors. Equipped with an end door 7' wide, its inside length was 70'1''. The Brake System was UC and its average weight was 136,000 lbs. The 6 wheeled trucks were truck class L-4x (straight equalizer). *(Dick Kuelbs)*

▲ Grey NYC 9110 was a 70' Baggage from Lot 2180 at Harrisburg, Pa. well into Penn Central ownership on 6-10-72. Numbers 9100-9199 were built by ACF in 1946-47 with 8' and 6' side doors, and an 8' wide end door. With a D22 Brake system, the all grey car had T-5-XR trucks.
(C.T. Bossler)

▼ Suited out in the classic two-tone grey, NYC 9152 was a 70' baggage from Lot 2180 at Dallas, Tex. on 5-11-63. Numbers 9100-9199 were from ACF order number 2910 equipped with truck class T-5 XR. (Dick Kuelbs)

NYC 5021 *Alonzo B. Cornell* was built by Budd in 1941 for EMPIRE STATE EXPRESS service. Numbers 5021-5022 had the famous Budd stainless steel fluted carbody. Mate 5022 was named *John A. Dix*. The 85' cars had a 60' main section and a 21' baggage section. The 36'' dia. wheels were in class T-2-XR trucks. Alonzo B. Cornell was a (Republican) Governor of New York State from 1880 to 1882.   *(George Ford)*

NYC 4814 was photographed at Mott Haven, NY on 11-29-66. Number 4810-4814 (Lot 796) were built by Pressed Steel Car Co. in 1911 with a 60' mail section and 4 wheeled trucks (Truck class R).   *(J.W. Swanberg)*

NYC 4915 from Lot 821 was at St. Louis on 5-4-67. With truck class K-2 (6-wheel drop equalizer), it was originally built as B&A 922 by Laconia Car Co. in 1913.

(Dick Kuelbs)

▲ Milk car NYC 6651 was part of Lot 2123 and at Dallas (UT) on 3-10-62. The milk car group 6611-6660 was built in 1931 by MDT in East Rochester.   *(Dick Kuelbs)*

▼ NYC 9672 was a former milk car converted into a Baggage-Express car. Shown at Fort Worth, Texas on the Texas & Pacific 12-24-61, it was classed as an SUF Car.
    (Dick Kuelbs)

NYC 9328 was another conversion. The 50'7'' Baggage Express (Lot 2206) is shown at Fort Worth (T&P) on 12-24-61. The group 9200-9399, were converted from troop sleepers, (Order no. 6753) at Pullman-Standard in 1945-46. They were re-conditioned at DSI during 1947-48. NYC 9328 is pictured in the original two-tone grey. *(Dick Kuelbs)*

The crew rides the point of NYC 9398 another member of Lot 2206 at Detroit in August 1963. Number 9398 has recently lost its two-tone grey scheme in the early 1960s simplication of passenger paint schemes. Note how the windows and end doors of the original troop sleeper have been sealed shut. *(Emery Gulash)*

The literal "end of the line" for NYC 9483, a 50'7'' Baggage Express (Lot 2230) came in So. Modena, Pa. just after 2-8-70 when it was photographed. Number 9400-9499 were order no. 6704 at Pullman-Standard in 1943-44. These troop sleepers for WWII were also converted at DSI in 1949. Their brake systems were AB-1-B; trucks ASF with A-3 ride control and 33'' wheels; and equipped with 110 volt AC plug-in lighting. The original troop sleeper trucks were Allied Full Cushion replaced with A-3 when Allied trucks were prohibited in interchange. *(C.T. Bossler)*

Coaches

NYC had a standard 70-foot coach comparable to PRR's famous P-70. 1428 cars were constructed between 1912 (Lot 801) and 1930 (Lot 2094) from seven different car builders according to NYC Specification 700. NYC 2241 is an example on Train #44 - a West Shore train at Bogota, NJ in April 1957. The former "Big Four" #900 was constructed by Standard Steel Co. in 1924.   *(Al Holtz)*

Since the early 1940s commuter coaches like NYC 853 were painted in "Pacemaker Green" - a DuPont paint similar to Pullman Green. The lettering and numbering was in imitation gold. Number 853 trailed West Shore Train #42 in April 1957. Part of Lot 2077, it was originally Lot 745, a steel underframe car. Rebuilt with a steel body by ACF in 1928, its wood interior was retained.   *(Al Holtz)*

In 1953 the Central started to paint its commuter coaches equipped with air conditioning into two tone gray sides, solid dark gray ends, black roof, underframe and trucks. NYC 2378 on a commuter train at White Plains, NY in 1962 was part of Lot 998 built by Osgood Bradley Car Company in 1926.   *(Al Holtz)*

Early coach lots had 6 wheeled trucks. NYC 943 on West Shore Train #66 at Bogota, NJ in April 1957 is an example. Original Lot 776 steel underframe, it was rebuilt by ACF in 1929. Only 4 wheel trucked cars had AC. With 6-wheel trucks, these rebuilt cars were not identical in dimensions to the Sp. 700 std. coach. *(Al Holtz)*

NYC 1996 a 70' coach from Lot 907 was at Mott Haven, NY on 11-30-66. Built by ACF in 1921, the two tone gray car originally had 86 seats and 1 toilet for commuter service. About 1961 Beech Grove shops upgraded these cars for commuter service - about 90 completed by the PC merger. Original wooden window frames were replaced by double panes of dark green glass in a rubber mounting.

(J.W. Swanberg)

P&LE 439 was a 70' coach from Lot 995 shown far from Pittsburgh at Brewster, NY on 2-18-68. Numbers 436-445 were built by Pressed Steel Car Co. in 1926. Pittsburgh & Lake Erie coaches had metal (brass) window sashes, 20 windows per side. With 80 seats, they had 2 toilets, (Men BL corner, Women AL corner). Their average weight was 143,000 pounds with a UC Brake system.

(J.W. Swanberg)

Boston & Albany 566 was built by Pullman in 1926 in Lot 2030. Shown at Brewster, NY in September 1956, all B&A coaches were numbered into the NYC system in 1957. Their average weight was 146,000 pounds with a UC Brake system. All B&A cars built after 1921 had 88 seats.

(J.W. Swanberg)

Steam escapes from NYC 2035, originally NYC 1088, a suburban coach from Lot 933 at Toledo, Ohio in February 1972. Built in 1923 by Standard Steel, the 88 seat coach had a two passenger bulkhead seat in the BR corner, one toilet and 4-wheeled trucks (R-7-X). The two tone gray car also had modernized windows.

(Dwight A. Smith)

Seventy foot long P&LE 445 from Lot 995 sits outside P&LE station Pittsburgh, Pa. in July 1972. P&LE 436-456 constituted Lot 995 built by Pressed Steel Car Co. in 1926. Equipped with 80 seats and 2 toilets, they had UC Brake Systems. P&LE coaches with air conditioning used a "C" under road number. This was the last P&LE coach in service.

(R.D. Cupper, E. Roy Ward collection)

▲ P&LE 452 from Lot 2032 at P&LE station in Pittsburgh in July 1971 was built by ACF in 1927. It had 80 seats, 2 toilets and UC brakes with an average weight of 143,000 pounds. (P&LE 170-183 and 400-470 were standard 70' coaches built by several builders). Like the other NYC subsidiaries, P&LE used "New York Central System" on letterboards. *(E. Roy Ward)*

▼ TH&B #74, a coach for the joint CP/NYC operation, is shown at Hamilton, Ontario in June 1968. With paired windows and 6 wheeled trucks, #74 shows the dual personality of the Toronto Hamilton & Buffalo's two owners - NYC and Canadian Pacific. *(Dwight A. Smith)*

NYC 1170 was a commuter coach from Lot 2065 at Boston, Ma., on 2-22-70. The 100 seat 1170 was former B&A 370 built by Osgood Bradley in 1927. There were 80 cars in Lots 969, 990, 2065 and 16 cars made it into the PC roster. *(J.W. Swanberg)*

B&A 374 a commuter coach from Lot 2065 was at Framingham, Ma. on an icy 4-8-56. B&A #300-379 were built by Osgood Bradley in 1925-1928 and renumbered 1100-1179 in 1957. The length was 78'-11¾'' and equipped with UC Brakes and truck class S-XR. *(W.T. Clynes)*

Stainless Steel NYC 3010 from Lot 2169 was at Rochester, NY in October 1966. Numbers 3000-3152 were constructed by Pullman-Standard in 1946. With an average weight of 122,000 pounds, its brake system was D-22-P and trucks, R-10-XR. *(Dave McKay)*

Another member of Lot 2169, NYC 3057 was at the western end of the NYC System, St. Louis on May 4, 1967. The cars had 64 seats, a Men's lavatory with 2 toilets, and a Women's lavatory with 1 toilet.

(Dick Kuelbs)

Lot 2169 coach #3123 is switched by the CP at Windsor Station, Montreal in April 1968. The car was in MONTREAL LIMITED service for the D&H/NYC.   *(Dwight A. Smith)*

A close up view of the same NYC 3123, this time at Toledo, Ohio on 9-16-67. It had been "de-fluted" in order to correct the wet conditions which plagued many Pullman-Standard cars underneath their stainless steel fluting.   *(David McKay)*

▲ In 1966, Beech Grove began to convert 64-seat Lot 2169 cars into 108-seat commuter coaches. Numbered into the 1715-1739 series, NYC 1722 is an example of Lot 2265 at Brewster, NY on 9-11-66. The "new" flat sides were painted exterior grey with a grey/blue window stripe.
(J.W. Swanberg)

▼ Fresh NYC 1730 another Lot 2265 conversion from Lot 2169 was at Mott Haven, NY on 11-30-66. Of the series 1715-1739—1723, 1725, 1729, 1732, 1733 retained their fluting; the balance had flat side sheets. *(J.W. Swanberg)*

▲ NYC 3608 was also from Lot 2169, shown in Philadelphia, Pa. at the Army-Navy game 12-2-72. Numbers 3600-3639 were assigned to "Empire Service." They were originally from the 3000-3152 group built by Pullman in 1946.   (C.T. Bossler)

▼ Two-tone grey NYC 2666 from Lot 2141 was on the westbound WOLVERINE at Kalamazoo, Mi., 9-67. Numbers 2645-2669 were built by ACF in 1941-42 with 56 seats, D-22-P brake system, and R-6-XR trucks.
(Emery Gulash)

▲ NYC 284 from Lot 2170 was at Mott Haven, NY on 11-29-66. Group 280-295 were built at ACF in 1947 with an average weight of only 115,000 lbs. because of its aluminum body. Their brake systems were D-22-P, with a R-10-XR truck on the passenger end and a T-4-XR truck on the baggage end. Only cars 280-283 had both Men's and Women's restrooms.   *(J.W. Swanberg)*

▼ Lot 2170 NYC 2803 served as a crew rider when photographed on Train #104 on July 5, 1968. Group 2800-2803 had fluted outside sheathing and 6' doors.

(George Ford)

Sleepers, parlors, etc.

NEW YORK CENTRAL SYSTEM

▲ NYC 10025, *Queensboro Bridge* from Lot 2211 was at Toledo, Ohio on 5-17-67. The 4-4-2 (4-compartment - 4 double bedroom - 2 drawing room) Pullman built in 1938 was one of 14 cars re-named to the ''Bridge'' series in 1949 for 20TH CENTURY LIMITED service. Its original name was *Imperial Bay*. *(J.W. Swanberg)*

▼ Fellow Lot 2211 Pullman *Rip Van Winkle Bridge* was shot at Dallas Union Terminal in Texas on 5-13-62. Painted in Illinois Central colors, nine ''Imperial'' cars were later purchased by the Atlantic Coast Line RR in 1962. This particular car became ACL *Kissimee River*. *(Dick Kuelbs)*

▲ NYC 10017 *Imperial Manor* from Lot 2219 was at Dallas, Tex. (UT) on 5-11-63. Built by Pullman in 1939 as *Imperial Estate*, it was re-named *Imperial Manor* to avoid confusion with the car *Imperial State*.   *(Dick Kuelbs)*

▼ NYC 10004, *Imperial Jewel* Lot 2219, was at Paoli, Pa. six years before Penn Central on 4-29-62. The 33 cars in group 10000-10033 were built by Pullman in 1939 and renumbered in 1952.   *(Dick Kuelbs)*

▲ NYC 10534, *Ashtabula County* Lot 2224, was at Toledo on 4-23-67. The 13 Double Bedroom Car was built at Pullman in 1940, part of an order for 22 cars in group 10530-10551 (all in the *County* group). The car was eventually sold to Ringling Bros. in 1967. *(David McKay)*

▼ NYC 10537, *Elkhart County,* from Lot 2220 at Toledo on 5-27-67 was a 13 Double Bedroom car built by Pullman in 1939. All the cars were renumbered in 1952 and this one was also eventually sold to Ringling Bros. in 1967 for circus train service. *(David McKay)*

NYC 10354 *Boothbay Harbor* was a 22 roomette car of Lot 2199 shown at Syracuse, NY 10-3-67. Built by Budd in 1949, there were 31 cars in the *Harbor* series (10350-10380). Number 10354 was sold down south in 1967 to the National Railways of Mexico.   *(J.W. Swanberg)*

NYC 10357 *Cape Vincent Harbor* from Lot 2199 was at Rochester, NY in October 1961. This 22 roomette Budd was sold to NdeM in 1966 and re-named *Presq Infiernillo*.

(David McKay)

NYC 10358 *Charlotte Harbor* also came from Lot 2199 and is shown at Englewood Station on 7-16-66. Eight cars from this group were converted to Sleeper Coaches by Budd in 1962 but #10358 joined other NYC alumni on the NdeM.   *(David McKay)*

▲ NYC 10143, *Portage River* Lot 2190, was at Toledo, Ohio 5-17-68. Built by Pullman-Standard in 1948, the 10 Roomette 6 Double Bedroom car was Pullman Plan 4123. Its average weight was 139,000 lbs, with a D-22-P Brake System, T-6-XR Trucks and 78'6'' Inside Length.

(J.W. Swanberg)

▼ NYC 10191, *Ausable River* from Lot 2190 was ''White-Lined'' for disposition in Toledo Ohio 5-17-68. The 10-6 Pullman-Standard product of 1948 was part of a group (10140-10236) of 97 cars. This was considered a very large order for lightweight Pullmans. *(J.W. Swanberg)*

NYC 10114, *Pine Valley* Lot 2200 was at Mott Haven, NY on 12-1-66. The 10 Roomette-6 Double Bedroom car was built by Budd in 1949. The stainless steel carbody preserved it well and it eventually became PC 4259, then Amtrak 2835 and was finally scrapped in 1976.

(J.W. Swanberg)

NYC 10125 *Meadow Valley* Lot 2200 was photographed in Cleveland, Ohio in August 1966. The group 10100-10139 consisted of 40 cars all in the *Valley* series. *Meadow Valley* also made a one-way trip south to serve the NdeM.   *(David McKay)*

Happy Valley NYC 10133 from Lot 2200 was at Englewood Station 7-16-66. The *Valley* series 10-6 Budd-built sleepers had T-6-XR (Vest. End) trucks and R-10-XR (Stub End) trucks.   *(Dave McKay)*

NYC 10507 *Port of Windsor* from Lot 2193 was at Englewood Station 7-16-66. The 12 Double Bedroom Pullman-Standard product of 1949 was from a group of 14 cars (10500-10513) in the *Port* series. No. 10507 was sold in 1968 to the Lake Shore Chapter of the NRHS.

(David McKay)

Also in Lot 2193, NYC 10510 *Port Clinton* was at Elkhart, Ind. on combined #25-27 when photographed on 11-7-67. The 12 Double Bedroom Pullman-Standard product of 1949 was built to Pullman Plan 4125. Its average weight was 137,000 pounds; Brake system D-22-P; and Trucks T-6-XR.   *(J.W. Swanberg)*

Sleeper-Lounge NYC 10626 *Woodland Stream* from Lot 2201 was at Cleveland, Ohio in August 1966. The 6 Double Bedroom-Buffet-Lounge was built at Budd in 1949. The *Stream* series (10620-10630) had 11 cars in the group. This one later became PC 4412, then Amtrak 3202.

(David McKay)

Sleeper-Coach NYC 10815 from Lot 2254 was at Cleveland, Ohio in August 1966. The 16 single room - 10 double room car was formerly the *South Haven Harbor*. It was part of a group (10810-10819) of 10 cars converted by Budd in 1962 from Lot 2199. *(David McKay)*

Heavyweight pullman MP34 rides the rear of Train #316 MOTOR CITY SPECIAL Chicago to Detroit in May 1946. The 12 section Pullman Car was in NYC service on the Michigan Division. *(Emery Gulash)*

NYC 82, *Herbert H. Lehman* from Lot 2145 was at Rochester, NY in October 1966. Built for EMPIRE STATE EXPRESS service by Budd in 1941, the car had 30 Parlor seats and a Drawing Room. Cars 81-86 (6 cars in group) had D-22-P Brake systems and a stainless steel body. *(David McKay)*

▲ NYC 400 was a full length dining car from Lot 2185 at Englewood station on 7-16-66. The Pullman-Standard product of 1948 was coupled to Kitchen Lounge Car #476. With an average weight of 119,700 lbs., its Brake style was D-22-P and trucks R-10-XR. The car survived into Penn Central ownership as PC #4584 but was declined by Amtrak and scrapped in 1971. *(David McKay)*

▼ Grill Diner NYC 461 from Lot 2178 was at Chicago in 1968. Cars 450-466 were stainless steel Budd products of 1948 with average weight of 132,000 lbs., D-22-P brake systems and T-6-XR trucks. This car became Penn Central 4561 and then Amtrak 8336. *(William F. Herrmann)*

▲ Commuter Club NYC #97 from Lot 956 was at Brewster, NY on 2-18-68. The former #2211 was built by Standard Steel Car Co. in 1924, and converted from a coach at Beech Grove in 1948. The 70' car had 50 seats, a kitchen, UC Brakes, R-7-X trucks and weighed 141,000 pounds. As the name implies, it spent its later life as a "member's only" private car for those commuters from exclusive Westchester communities that worked in the Big Apple.

(J.W. Swanburg)

▼ Another favorite "hangout" for commuters was Bar Counter #1599 from Lot 2020 shown at Brewster, NY, also on 2-18-68. Built by Pullman in 1926 (Order 4948) as Dining Car #405, it had been converted in 1958 for Michigan TIMBERLINER service. After that service ceased, it was transferred to New York for Hudson and Harlem Division service. With an inside length of 73'6", it weighed in at a hefty 179,100 pounds and rode on K-5-AX trucks.

(J.W. Swanburg)

Observation cars

▲ NYC #1019 trails THE MERCURY through Dearborn, Michigan back in March 1941. Named *Detroit*, the 36-seat Parlor-Observation had been converted in 1936 for MERCURY service after having been built by Osgood-Bradley Co. in 1927. Lot 2038 consisted of 30 suburban coaches.
(Emery Gulash)

▼ Train #75, THE MERCURY whips through Wayne, Michigan in 1941. Eighteen of the coaches were rebuilt for THE MERCURY in 1936 and 1939 after having been originally used on the Putnam Division. In addition 80 of these suburban coaches were built for B&A service.
(Emery Gulash)

▲ A stainless steel jewel glistens in the sun on display at Erie, PA 12-6-1941. The next morning the festive mood would be shattered as the world was startled by the news from Pearl Harbor.   *(William F. Herrmann collection)*

▼ Built by Budd earlier in 1941 and matched up with a similarly fluted Hudson the new EMPIRE STATE EXPRESS was a strikingly handsome train. Equipped with a R-6-XR front truck, R-8-XR rear truck and clasp brakes, this car was the *Franklin D. Roosevelt.*
(William F. Herrmann collection)

Hickory Creek brings up the markers on Train #25 at Elkhart, Ind. Station on 11-7-67. The Observation-Lounge - 5 Double Bedroom car was built specially for the 20TH CENTURY LIMITED and placed in service 9-15-48. It was part of Lot 2194.

(J.W. Swanberg)

The same NYC 10570 *Hickory Creek* shows its other side at Englewood Station 9-12-64. The distinctive observation had no rear doors and a distinctive zig-zag in the lightning stripe to get around the extra large lounge windows. The car had a T-6XR truck on the vestibule end and R-10XR truck on the observation end.

(David McKay)

Trains 25 and 26 traversed most of their New York-Chicago route during the night. This is Toledo Union Station in 1965 as the eastbound 20TH CENTURY LIMITED pauses as a few passengers linger on in the lounge before retiring. After a few hours of rest, they would awaken to the morning light reflecting off the majestic Hudson River.

(William F. Herrmann collection)

▲ The twin to *Hickory Creek* was *Sandy Creek* shown here on Train #25 at Gary, Ind. 8-12-67. NYC 10634 was the other part of Lot 2194 and had the same trucks as 10633 *Hickory Creek*. (David McKay)

▼ *Sandy Creek* on the 20TH CENTURY LIMITED sticks out at LaSalle St. Station, Chicago on 7-22-65. This was morning, the end of the trip for Train 25 and *Sandy Creek* would be washed thoroughly, serviced and turned for its afternoon departure on #26, the eastbound 20TH CENTURY. (J.W. Swanberg)

▲ The interior of NYC 10566 *Wingate Brook* was recorded on the sad occasion of the last run of 20TH CENTURY LIMITED in December 1967. Lot 2204 was built by Budd in 1949 and had the same trucks as Lot 2194.

(William F. Herrmann collection)

▼ NYC #67 was from Lot 2177 and shown here at Toledo, Ohio on 3-17-68. Budd-built in 1948, cars 58-70 where Parlor Observations, part of Budd Lot 9638-004.

(J.W. Swanberg)

▲ NYC #66 also from Lot 2177 at Harmon in March 1965. As passenger deficits increased and train amenities were reduced, observations such as #66 became nuisances to the railroad, handicapped by their special features. *(Bob Hart)*

▼ An unrecorded member of Lot 2177 pauses at Port Henry on 2-27-65. The stainless steel Budd Company product of 1948 was in joint NYC/D&H LAURGENTIAN service between New York City and Montreal. *(George Ford)*

▲ NYC #30, an Official Inspection car rests at Albany, NY in September 1965. First the *Queen Elizabeth* then the *Hudson River* the car was used on the EMPIRE STATE EXPRESS until the train was streamlined. Built by PC&M in 1925 (Lot 4862 plan 3957), it had 26 chairs and a drawing room. Purchased in 1942 by NYC, it became *Kalamazoo River* and used on Michigan Central's TWILIGHT in 1942. In 1952 it became #30, went to PC also as #30, and then to Conrail as #10.   *(George Ford)*

▼ Business Car NYC #3 was at Syracuse, NY 10-3-67. The 74' car was built by PC&M in May 1928 (Lot 2047) and was originally assigned to Harold Vanderbilt. In 1927-1928 Pullman delivered steel heavyweight business cars NYC 1-5, B&A 99, MC-1, CCC&STL 400 and P&LE 99 to replace older wooden cars.   *(J.W. Swanberg)*

From 1946 to 1966 NYC converted eighty-one 70 foot coaches into rider coaches. Blanking 12 windows on each side, the road removed seats in center and installed oil stoves and fuel tanks, re-numbering the cars into the 2700-series. This example trails a *Flexi Van* train on the Boston and Albany on April 26, 1971.

(George Ford)

A close-up of NYC 2726 at Chicago in 1968 exemplifies Lot 884. Originally built by Barney & Smith in 1918 as a coach, it was transformed forty years later in 1958 into this rider coach.   *(William F. Herrmann)*

NYC 2712 from Lot 958 at Detroit on 9-23-69. Built by ACF in 1924, it was converted from a coach in 1964 and now was technically Penn Central property.   *(J.W. Swanberg)*

Stock cars

▲ In line with most other railroads, the New York Central's stock trade was evaporating during the 1950's and 60's due to improved refrigeration and trucking. To handle its limited business in the Sixties, the Central utilized NISX (North American Car Corp) stock cars leased to NYC. As of 8/1/67, they were NISX 2000-2056 (57 cars SM 40T single deck) and NISX 3000-3149 (89 cars SF 40T double deck). This was double deck NISX 3039 down in Fort Worth, Texas in July 1965 for another load of hogs or sheep. *(Dick Kuelbs)*

▼ NISX 3121 is pictured at Cleveland on April 6, 1968. With an inside length of 50'0'', the car had a capacity of 80,000 lbs. *(David McKay)*

Refrigerator cars

▲ NYC 86942 a wood refrigerator car was at Lansing, Michigan in 1946. The 50'6'' car was in wheel service for shipping auto wheels from Motor Wheel Corp. in Lansing to auto plants. The insulated cars provided temperature stability when warm auto wheels were loaded in the winter. Lot 756-B (86400-86707 & 86930-86999 - 78 cars) were converted from MDT Refrigerators in 1946.

(Emery Gulash)

▼ NYRX 3026 (group 3000-3099) was on the Katy RR at Dallas 6-9-67. The RBL class car's overall length was 42'3'', with a capacity of 100,000 lbs. Its inside length was 40'0'', inside width 9'2'' with a crushed ice capacity of 5900 lbs. *(Dick Kuelbs)*

▲ NYMX 1037 a mechanical refrigerator car was near Albany in August 1972. New in 1956, its overall length was 52'5" capacity 120,000 pounds, inside length was 44'5½" and inside width 8'6". The group 1000-1099 was painted with yellow sides and a dark blue band. On this example in PC days, the 45"x30" NYC oval had been painted out. *(George Ford)*

▼ NYRX 2507 was a class RB refrigerator at Fort Worth, Texas in August 1961. Adorned with an "Early Bird" Herald, its overall length was 41'10", capacity 100,000 lbs., inside length 40'0" and inside width 9'0". It was part of group 2500-2599. *(Dick Kuelbs)*

▲ MDT 12322 was at Dallas (MKT) on 5-21-61. Its overall length was 42'6", capacity 70,000 lbs., inside length 33'2¾" and inside width 8'3" equipped with air circulating fans. The stencil "Return to Weehawken NJ" implies banana service. *(Dick Kuelbs)*

▼ MDT 11440 was at Derby, Maine for potato loading on BAR 7-25-70. The group 11000-13999 constituted class RB. *(J.W. Swanberg)*

NYC 749592 was a gondola from Lot 791G at Reading, PA 6-23-70. Group 749590-749601 was built 10-49 by Greenville. Equipped with a steel cover, its capacity was 140,000.

(C.T. Bossler)

65'6'' long P&LE 16062 was part of Lot 878-G built in 1957-58 by Greenville. Photographed at Sinns, PA in August 1972, its capacity was 140,000 lbs. Group 16000-16499 consisted of 500 cars. *(E. Roy Ward)*

Another example of Lot 878-G P&LE 16461 was at Ft. Worth, Texas 10-23-71. The 70 ton gondola had a lightweight of 67,600 lbs.

(Dick Kuelbs)

▲ P&LE 18000 shown at East Rochester, NY on 1-20-67 was the sample car for Lot 116-G. Despatch Shops went on to construct 499 more whose inside length was 65'6''.
(J.W. Swanberg)

▼ P&LE 18129 heads up a string on new Lot 116-G gons at East Rochester, NY 2-67. Group 18000-18499 had steel floors and fixed ends. *(J.W. Swanberg)*

▲ Decked out in fresh "Jade Green," P&LE 17243 was at Dallas Union Terminal (Texas Pacific) on 7-30-67. Built two months earlier by Greenville in May 1967, Lot 117-G (17000-17249) had a capacity 142000 lbs. The first green box car (with black roof and ends) came out of Despatch Shops on 11-19-58. Central termed this "Century Green." The 1958 date is important to model railroaders; since Central dieselization was completed in May 1957, running jade green box cars behind NYC steam is an anachronism.

(Dick Kuelbs)

▼ P&LE 18414 was also new in 1967 (Lot 123-G Despatch Shops) but wore the more usual NYC black. Shown at Dallas on 7-7-68, the inside length of 52'6'' held a load of pipe.

(Dick Kuelbs)

Another 1967 product of Despatch Shops, NYC 744048 was 56'11'' long (Lot 148G). Photographed at East Reading, PA yard the 100 ton hot steel coil and slat gon had no oval. Its entire body was painted with high temperature black paint with no stencils above the floor line. Group 744000-744049 had a capacity of 190,000 lbs.

(C.T. Bossler)

NYC 745054 was from Lot 130-G and at Etowah, Tenn. (on L&N) in June 1976. Built 6-67 for hot steel slab loading, it also had no stencils above floor line. The group 745000-745249 consisted of 250 cars, all built at Despatch Shops. *(Ed Stoll)*

The fixed ends of NYC 613043 protruded above the sides for use in hauling special commodities like pipe. The burned off paint and lettering on this car is a good example of the reason the other two cars on this page carried their stencils below the floor line. NYC 613043 was at Gary, Indiana, source of much steel loading for the Central, in May 1967.

(Emery Gulash)

NYC 481664 was at Thorndale, PA April 14, 1973. Part of Lot 690F, the 52' flat car had been constructed 32 years earlier at Despatch Shops.

(C.T. Bossler)

NYC 499706 from Lot 721F was at Coatesville, PA on 8-20-76. 53'6'' flats 499600-499799 were built by DSI in 1943. With 70 ton trucks, 33'' wheels, 6x11 journals, they had a short bulkhead on one end.

(C.T. Bossler)

NYC 481134 equipped with bulkheads was from Lot 793F shown at Coatesville, PA 2-21-76. The FMS flat (481100-481134) was converted in 1954 with 6'6'' bulkheads (projects 316, 318, 319). The car was 48'6'' between bulkheads. *(C.T. Bossler)*

NYC 499092 was a 4-truck flat (four wheel trucks) from Lot 835F shown at Reading, PA, 11-26-74. With a capacity of 333,000 pounds, its overall length was 70'0'' and a depressed center portion 25' long. The group 499089-499092 was built at DSI in 1952. *(C.T. Bossler)*

NYC 506089 was a 53'6'' FM flat from Lot 888F. One of 200 cars built by Pullman-Standard in 1960, it had all-welded construction, wood floor, and 70-ton trucks with 33'' wheels. The NYC paint was holding up twenty years after the demise of the Central when this carload of pipe was photographed west of Enola, PA in Conrail freight ENPIOW. *(H.E. Brouse)*

P&LE 625 had jade green on its 53'6'' length when photographed at Thorndale, PA 4-14-73. Lot 951F (600-699 100 cars) was built at Greenville 10-64. With 70 ton trucks, cushion underframe, 12'' high bulkhead at each end, 14 stake pockets per side, two on each end, 13 loading strap anchors on each side between pockets, it also had a wood floor 10'6'' wide. *(C.T. Bossler)*

▲ NYC 752017 a coil steel trough car from Lot 984F was at Wayne, Mi. December 1966. The 100 cars (752000-752099) in this group built by Evans had 100-ton trucks, two hoods, two 23'4'' long troughs, 8 adjustable crossbars, and Hydra-Cushion with 20'' travel. *(Emery Gulash)*

▼ P&LE 42181 was a very similar coil steel trough car from Lot 110F. Photographed at Port Vue, PA on March 5, 1975, it was enjoying its last years of activity as soon the P&LE would see its signature steel traffic all but disappear. *(E. Roy Ward)*

P&LE 42256 was a coil steel ''bread box'' trough car at Reading, PA 6-27-70. One of 50 cars (42250-42299) built by Evans in 1967, it was part of Lot 111F. *(C.T. Bossler)*

P&LE 42252 is a good side example of GBSR Lot 111F ''bread box'' car at Dallas on July 4, 1971. With a huge 50' trough, 125 ton trucks, cushion underframe, and eight adjustable crossbars, the car had a ''super'' load limit of 231,600 lbs and a light weight of 83,400 lbs. *(Dick Kuelbs)*

NYC 481405 was a Bulkhead Flat (FMS) photographed in September 1961. As of 8/1/67 there were 266 converted cars in series IHB 8002-8096 and NYC 481000-499682 from Lots 712-F, 721-F, 722-F and 793-F. *(Collection of Dick Kuelbs)*

NYC 498996 was from Lot 898-F and at Ft. Worth, Tex (on FW&D) 7-30-61. The two 6-wheel trucked, depressed center flat had a capacity of 245000 pounds and overall length of 60'10''. The depressed center portion was 21' long. The group consisted of 498991-498996. *(Dick Kuelbs)*

NYC 753009 from Lot 122F was at Reading, PA 4-7-71. Group 753000-753204 (205 cars) was built at Greenville 8/67. This was a coil steel ''hoodless'' trough car with 125 ton trucks and cushion underframe. *(C.T. Bossler)*

NYC 498989 from Lot 126F was at Thorndale, PA 7-13-75. With a capacity of 400,000 lbs, its overall length was 77'7''. The 4 truck flat (depressed center) was part of group 498986-498989. *(C.T. Bossler)*

Covered hoppers

NEW YORK CENTRAL SYSTEM

▲ A fresh NYC 881182 Lot 680H covered hopper rests at Detroit in 1955. The 70 ton 1800 cu. ft. car was from group 880700-881199 built at Despatch Shop in 1940. The 32' long gray car wore a 28¼''x19⅛'' NYC oval. The load limit was 155800 lbs. and road weight 54,200 lbs.
(Emery Gulash)

▼ Thirty-seven year old NYC 881844 from Lot 747H has a much more "used" appearance at Northumberland, PA well into Conrail ownership on 2-27-83. Group 881200-881949 was constructed at DSI in 1946. *(H.E. Brouse)*

NYC 882368 from Lot 843H was at Reading, PA 4-14-71. The two pocket car group 882050-882649 was built at Pullman-Standard (Mich City, IN) in 1953. The 35' long car had 70 ton trucks and was painted gray with a 28¼'' x 19⅛'' oval. *(C.T. Bossler)*

NYC 883227 was also at Reading, PA 5-26-78. The 500 cars of Lot 860H (883100-883499) were built at Pullman-Standard (Butler, PA) in March 1956. These two pocket gray cars had 29'' x 19⅜'' ovals and eight round hatches. Some cars were lined.
(C.T. Bossler)

Central subsidiary P&LE 1365 was at Wyomissing, PA on March 12, 1978. The 250 cars from Lot 873H (1300-1549) were constructed by ACF in 1957. Some of these cars were also lined. *(C.T. Bossler)*

A weathered P&LE 1595 from Lot 874H was at Corsicana, TX 8-13-78. The group 1550-1699 was built at Pullman-Standard (Butler, PA) in 1957. The two pocket 35' long cars had 8 round roof hatches and a capacity of 2003 cu. ft. *(Dick Kuelbs)*

P&LE 1770 a 70 ton covered hopper from Lot 875H was home in Pittsburgh in August 1979. The 1957 group 1700-1799 consisted of 100 cars built by Pullman Standard in nearby Butler, PA. The cars were 47-0¾ long over strikers and rode on 70 ton friction bearing trucks.

(Michael Bradley)

Three pocket NYC 885053 was at Garland, TX in November 1971. The 75 cars from Lot 892H (885000-885074) were built by Pullman-Standard (Butler, PA) in June 1960. With 47' in length they could hold 3506 cu. ft. on their 50 ton trucks.

(C.T. Bossler)

▲ NYC 885092 from Lot 893H was at Reading, PA in August 1982. Built in July 1960, the 25 cars (885075-885099) were constructed by Pullman-Standard in their Butler, PA plant. Equipped with pneumatic outlets, 10 round roof hatches and 70 ton trucks, the car had 3506 cu. ft. of capacity. *(C.T. Bossler)*

▼ NYC 885236 was a 3 pocket covered hopper from Lot 916H shot at So. Philadelphia, PA on 12-1-73. The LO group (885150-885299) had gravity-pneumatic outlets and 10 round roof hatches within its 47' length. *(C.T. Bossler)*

NYC 885900 was the unique member of Lot 923H shown at Northumberland, PA on 2-16-80. The one-of-a-kind car was built at ACF in 1961. Equipped with pneumatic outlets it had 6 roof hatches, a load limit of 195400 lbs, and lightweight of 67,600 lbs. The 97½ ton covered hopper was a "center flow" hopper.

(H.E. Brouse)

Brand new NYC 886108 a 4650 cu. ft. covered hopper was at Roberts Valley Road in October 1964. The 25 cars of Lot 954H (886097-886121) were built by ACF in 1964 with 6 round hatch covers and 100 ton trucks. Equipped with welded gravity outlets and car lining, it was painted light gray with black trucks and a huge 12'-0''x5'-4'' oval. This car carried the older style reporting marks.

(Wm. Echternacht, NRHS collection)

NYC 886305 from Lot 958H was at East Reading Yard 4-26-74. The 100 cars from group 886226-886325 were built by ACF in 1965. These lined cars had a continuous hatch arrangement.

(C.T. Bossler)

▲ *Flexi Flo* covered hopper NYC 885731 from Lot 996H was at Northumberland, PA 5-8-83. The 120 cars of group 885680-885799 were built by ACF at Milton, PA in 1966. Cement could be loaded/unloaded in these cars by creating a Pressure-Differential within via an air inlet. The big 6'6''x3'1'' NYC oval dressed up the light gray body and black trucks of the car. *(H.E. Brouse)*

▼ 4650 cubic foot capacity NYC 886756 was at Blandon, PA 5-5-70. Lot 114H (886726-886825) consisted of 100 cars built by American Car and Foundry at its Huntington, West Virginia plant in 1966. *(C.T. Bossler)*

▲ Super center flow NYC 892018 was a member of Lot 131H. These continuous hatch cars rode on 100-ton trucks.
(H.O. Preble, Emmons Lancaster collection)

▼ NYC 892138 was at Reading, PA 4-28-74. The 5700 cubic foot capacity Lot 131H (892000-892183) was built by ACF at Huntington, WV in September 1967.
(C.T. Bossler)

▲ NYC 886888 was from Lot 138H photographed at Northumberland, PA 2-27-83. The group 886826-887025 was built at Pullman-Standard at Butler, PA in 1967 with 24''x30'' gravity outlets and 100 ton trucks. With a light gray body and black trucks, the oval size was 4'4''x23½''. Note how the word ''System'' is cut in half on this herald.

(H.E. Brouse)

▼ You can't haul powdered cement around for five years and not have plenty of evidence of the service. NYC 885829 from Lot 963H was on the B&A at the *Flexi-Flo* Yard in Framingham, Mass 2-70. Built by ACF in 1965 with 125 ton trucks and 38'' wheels, the Pressure-Differential *Flexi-Flo* covered Hoppers from group 885825-885899 consisted of 75 cars.

(J. Emmons Lancaster)

Open-top hoppers

▲ Being shoved along in a ballast train, NYC 838490 was at MP 34 East of Ann Arbor, MI in 1946. The 1750 cars of Lot 412H (840250-841999) were built by American Car & Foundry, Berwick, PA in 1921. These cars were USRA Design Spec 1005, originally CCCS&L 80250-81999.

(Emery Gulash)

▼ A good example of the traditional ''red body'' NYC hopper of the 1940s and 50s. NYC 862543 from Lot 846H was at Lansing, Mich. in 1954. Lot 846H (862000-865499) was originally built by DSI in February 1940. In 1953 they were converted at Greenville Car Co. from Lot 676H receiving the new body with red paint and black hoppers and trucks. The car was stencilled ''Repacked 11-17-53'' which was also the date out of shop for the 55 ton, 2 pocket hopper.

(Emery Gulash)

▲ On February 20, 1941, the Central began to paint flat cars and open-top hoppers red instead of black (although the underside of hopper slope sheets remained black for several years). In the late 1950s, the NYC System switched back to all black for its coal hoppers. P&LE 4957 from Lot 772H exemplifies this at Reading, PA on April 19, 1974. The class HM car was built at DSI 11-48 in group 4000-4999 (1000 hoppers). *(C.T. Bossler)*

▼ 55 ton P&LE 4995 sits among other 50/55 ton hoppers in the Pittsburgh area in 1966. The fresh black paint of the Lot 772H hopper will soon gain an appearance more akin to its companions. *(Dick Kuelbs)*

P&LE 75778 strayed way down to Dallas, Texas on the Rock Island when photographed on Christmas Eve 1964. The HM class hopper from Lot 834H was part of the 1000 car group 75000-75999 built by Pullman-Standard at Butler, PA in 1952.
(Dick Kuelbs)

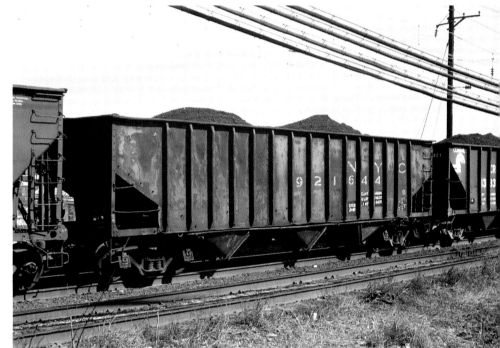

Three pocket NYC 921644 was at Enola, PA 3-15-81. Lot 865H (921520-922249) was built at DSI in 1960. The 70-ton class HT cars were 41'8'' long equipped with 70-ton friction bearing National C-1 trucks and Enterprise doors.
(H.E. Brouse)

NYC 950144 from Lot 904H was deep in PRR's territory at Radebaugh, PA in December 1972. The rivalry was supposed to be over now that it was Penn Central but we learned otherwise. Group 95000-950349 was built at DSI in 1961. It now had Enterprise longitudinal doors for ballast service.
(E. Roy Ward)

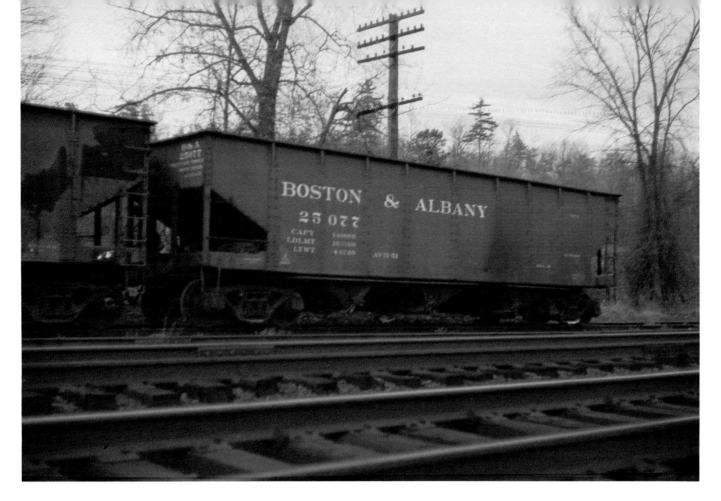

▲ B&A hoppers Lot 597-H were built by Standard Steel Car at Butler, PA in 1927. Nineteen years passed before NYC received another new 70 ton hopper and they were delivered in black paint.   *(Arthur Mitchell)*

▼ A nice ¾ view of NYC 831826 in January 1970. Lot 942H cars had a capacity of 2342 cubic feet of capacity and 32'6'' length over strikers.   *(Dick Kuelbs collection)*

▲ The NYC resurrected a long lost "paper railroad" subsidiary for equipment trust reasons when it stencilled some cars for Toledo and Ohio Central (TOC). TOC 830737 was another Lot 942H hopper. Shown at Sunbury, PA on 3-14-81, this class HM hopper was part of group 830500-830849 rebuilt in 1965 from 55 ton hoppers.   *(H.E. Brouse)*

▼ NYC 950468 was at Reading, PA 7-9-75. Lot 957H (950350-950499) consisted of 150 cars rebuilt in 1965 from 55-ton 2 pocket hoppers. Equipped with longitudinal hopper doors, the 2333 cu. ft. hopper was class HK.

(C.T. Bossler)

Intermodal/Automobile traffic

▲ As a major participant in the autoparts traffic to and from Detroit, the Central was quick to take advantage of the rack-equipped long flats which began to recoup new auto deliveries for the rail industry. MDAX 186 was at Dallas (UT-MKT) 12-22-61. The type ML tri-level flat was loaded with 15 Fords. The group 100-199 had an overall length 92'3''. *(Dick Kuelbs)*

▼ Empty MDAX 1149 was back at the Ford Co. at River Rouge, Mich. in December 1963 for another load. Type ML, Class TRI group 900-1499 had an overall length of 92'7''. *(Emery Gulash)*

▲ Bi-level MDAX 325 was photographed from above at Toledo, Ohio in August 1966 with a load of Jeeps.

(Emery Gulash)

▼ Some early bi-level flats were painted red before the switchover to jade green. This National Car Company NIFX car was at the River Rouge Ford Company yard in January 1961. Built only a month earlier in December 1960, the red car had a black 29''x19⅜'' NYC oval.

(Emery Gulash)

▲ A very nice overall photograph of a busy vintage scene at Chicago's La Salle Street Station in June 1961. Two short 35' NYC container vans share the spotlight with a Santa Fe express box car and an arriving Rock Island streamliner. *(Collection of Dick Kuelbs)*

▼ While almost the entire railroad industry was embracing the concept of "piggybacking" trailers complete with wheel assemblies aboard flat cars, the Central was advocating a concept of taking the van body-only for the ride, re-attaching a set of bogy wheels at the termination of the trip. Its container concept was dubbed *Flexi-Van*. Here one of the single-axle vans sets out on the road portion of its journey near Pershing Road, Weehawken, NJ 3-24-59. *(At Holtz)*

Mark IV *Flexi-Van* MFVX 6943 from Lot 2269 was built at Greenville in 1966-67 for passenger service. Shown at St. Louis 5-4-67 the *Flexi-Van* flat had two containers. Its length over strikers was 87' 11½'' with a load limit of 120,000 lbs. MFVX cars were leased from Merchants Despatch Trans. Co., a NYC property itself.

(Dick Kuelbs)

NYCU 203019 was a *Flexi-Van* used in US Mail service. Shown at Buffalo, NY in April 1970, the Penn Central did not look upon *Flexi-Van* in the same light as NYC and the service eventually evaporated.

(Edward J. Stroll)

NYCU 201177 was being loaded on to the flat at Detroit in July 1966. Note that the tractor was yellow in NYC days and jade green after PC took over. *(Emery Gulash)*

Box cars

▲ P&LE 30135 was a standard 40' single door box car built by Pressed Steel Car Co. in 1940. Photographed at Ft. Worth, TX 12-16-62, Lot 682B consisted of P&LE 30000-30499 (500 XM cars) with white logo and black background for the Central oval. *(Dick Kuelbs)*

▼ The box car red look became passé on the Central in the late 1958 changover to Century (jade) green. NYC 176272 was a 50' single door (8' door) car built by DSI in 1941 and photographed at Wayne Jct., PA 6-61. Lot 692B (NYC 176200-176799) had a height of 15'0 3/32 over running boards. *(R.S. Short)*

As an E8 with coupler shield in place passes in 1952, NYC 174020 shows off the vermillion and grey *Pacemaker* scheme. One of 1000 cars built by Despatch Shops Inc. in 1945 it was part of Lot 737B. Numbers 174000-174249 had Youngstown corrugated doors and Dreadnaught ends.

(Emery Gulash)

Train NB-1 made the *Pacemaker* first run on 7-1-46 from West 33rd Street New York City. The initial service was NB-1 and BN-2. In April 1949 the Central added the *New England Pacemaker* BB-1 and BB-2 between Boston and Buffalo. By 1971 when this photo was taken, *Pacemaker* service was but a distant memory but still the vermillion and gray paint stayed on. Black oval NYC 175058 had been renumbered from its original 174058 (its *Pacemaker* number) by simply changing the ''4'' into a ''5.'' *(George Ford)*

NYC 174942, a pristine example of *Pacemaker Fast Freight Service,* was from Lot 737B and at Pittsfield, Mass in March 1949. Number 174000-174999 had 6' wide doors on a 40'6'' long body built by DSI in 1945. Equipped with Barber high-speed trucks and all-white NYC oval, 174000-174249 had Youngstown corrugated doors and 174250-174999-Superior 7-panel doors.

(Mike Bullock)

▲ NYC 159895 was a 40' XM (6' doors) from Lot 734B at the B&A West Yard on 5/26/60. NYC 159000-159999 were built at DSI in 1944. Now decked out in Century green with black ends its load limit was 129,800 lbs.

(George Ford)

▼ NYC 75509 was a 50' double-door XM (15' door opening) from Lot 736B built by ACF in 1945. Numbers 74600-75999 had a load limit of 119,300 lbs. and lt. wt. of 57,700 lbs. *(Dick Kuelbs collection)*

▲ A string of four rebuilt NYC box cars await cereal box loading outside the Kellogg's plant at Battle Creek, Michigan in July 1959. NYC 177769 was an XM with 8'0'' door opening from Lot 742B built by ACF in 1945.

(Emery Gulash)

▼ The huge oval logo of NYC 162440 dominates the 40' single door XM car from Lot 743B shown at Corning, NY in November 1959. The group 162000-163999 were originally built by Despatch Shops and later overhauled and painted at Beech Grove shops in 1959. The Century green sides were accented with black ends and roof.

(David Conner)

Another NYC subsidiary represented in the reporting marks on various cars was Peoria & Eastern. P&E 3600 was a 40' single door box car shown at Dallas, Texas Union Terminal on the MKT on May 24, 1964.

(Dick Kuelbs)

The much better known subsidiary of NYC was P&LE which had a much larger car fleet than P&E. P&LE 36167 was a 40' single door box at Fort Worth, Texas in 1962.

(F.B. King, Dick Kuelbs collection)

P&LE 7458, a 50' single door XML was at Dallas, TX (UT-TP) on 11-28-63. Lot 921B consisted of 7300-7599 (300 cars) built by DSI in 1963. Equipped with cushion underframe (20'' travel), 10' door, 2 belt raids, the cars had load limits of 144800 lbs on their 70-ton trucks. *(Dick Kuelbs)*

A journeyman 40' box P&LE 35246 is waiting for the scrapper at Monnesson, PA 3-22-80. P&LE 35000-35899 (Lot 697B) was built by Pressed Steel Car Co. in 1941. By 1967, there were only 102 cars remaining.

(E. Roy Ward)

PLE 5425 was a 40' single door XM (6' wide door) at Fort Worth, Tex. 2-5-67. P&LE 5000-5999 (Lot 774B) were built at DSI in 1949 and decorated with a white logo complete with black ''Central'' band and a slogan ''Serves the Steel Centers.''

(Dick Kuelbs)

Twenty years after construction, a workhorse XM 40' single door box rests on the Schuylkill Valley Branch 5-23-70. NYC 169129 was part of group 169000-170499 (Lot 798B) built by Pullman in 1950. The PS-I was leased from Equitable Life Assurance Society. (C.T. Bossler)

▲ Nice truck detail shows up in the early light of November 24, 1960 as P&LE 20982 from Lot 800B sits at Dallas, TX on the MKT. P&LE groups 20000-20999 was constructed at DSI in 1950. About ½ of the cars (555) remained by 1974. *(Dick Kuelbs)*

▼ Also on the Katy at Dallas on May 14, 1961, P&LE 22300 was a Lot 819B 40' single door box. This group 22000-22999 was built at DSI in 1952 with 6' doors and a load limit of 130,000 lbs. *(Dick Kuelbs)*

▲ From the camera of the Central's official photographer, Ed Nowak, we see NYC 164203 at an unknown location and date. The 4x5'' transparency is captioned ''box car with Hi Speed trucks.'' A ''Star'' car built by DSI in October 1947 when this photo was taken, it was a member of Lot 759B (164000-164999—1000 cars).

(Ed Nowak, Morning Sun Books collection)

▼ Typical of how most NYC equipment survived the Penn Central era, NYC 71819 a 50' double door box was at Altoona, PA 5-20-74. Lot 820B (71500-71999) built at DSI in 1952 had only 66 cars remaining in 1974 when this photo was taken. With a door opening of 15'1¾'' load limit 91,000, lt. wt. 86000, its AAR description was ''XP.''

(C.T. Bossler)

▲ When the Century (jade) green was fresh and new, it made a very attractive paint scheme. 50' single door NYC 84456 was an example at Detroit, MI in October 1963. Lot 855B (84430-84474, 44 cars) was built at DSI in 1956. In 1963 they were converted for special service (Project P-393, 395) and assigned to Ford Motor Co.

(Emery Gulash)

▼ One of the more memorable of "boxcar red" boxcars seen across the country was NYC's fleet adorned with *Early Bird* circular yellow emblems. NYC 45390 from Lot 862B was at Detroit, Mi. in June 1957. The group 45000-46899 were plain-jane class XM box cars built by DSI that year of 1957 and assigned to auto parts service.

(Emery Gulash)

After almost 28 years of service NYC 46088 still advertises *Early Bird* service, although the Central had long since discontinued that campaign. Lot 862-B NYC 46088 was at the New Haven interchange at Maybrook, NY on May 15, 1965. *(George Ford)*

A good example of a Lot 860B car dressed up in Century green, NYC 87848 was stored at Derry, PA in June 1973 under PC ownership. Group 87791-87877 consisted of 87 cars, with 19 Belt Rails and stencil "SL" for Frigidaire (appliance) service. They were converted in 1967 for this special service - (Project P-66). *(E. Roy Ward)*

Also stored at Derry, PA that day in June 1973 was NYC 86905 another 50' Double Door box from Lot 862B. Group 86897-86966 consisted of 70 cars with 7 Belt Rails and an "SL" for Ford Parts. In 1961, they were converted for auto parts service (Project P-27) with a load limit of 106,600 lbs. *(E. Roy Ward)*

Peoria & Eastern 4532, a 50' single door car from Lot 883B, was at Detroit in May 1976. Group 4500-4544 (45 cars) were built at DSI in 1959 with a load limit of 118,000 lbs and 8' doors. *(Emery Gulash)*

P&LE 7124 a 50' single door car from Lot 897B was at Dallas, Tex (MKT) 4-16-67. First in the group 7100-7149, the class XML cars were built at DSI in 1961. Equipped with perforated steel floor plates, and Barber tube cushioning with 20'' travel, and 9 Belt rails the ''SL'' car had a load limit of 146,800 lbs. *(Dick Kuelbs)*

NYC 43663, a 50' double door box from Lot 907B, was on the PRR at Lemoyne, PA 5-4-62. Cars 43500-43947 were class XM cars built by DSI in 1961. With a 15-0¼ door opening, they had 50 ton trucks and a load limit of 114,800 lbs. The three photos on this page are an excellent illustration of the various sizes of oval Central emblems on Century green cars.

(Wm. Echternacht, NRHS collection)

Workhorse NYC 200495, a standard 40' single door box was at Ann Arbor, Mi. in February 1967. Lot 912B (200000-201499) was converted at the DSI E. Rochester Shops in 1962-63 from Lots 590, 594, and 610B which had been built in 1940-1946 as Lots 686, 688, and 738B. *(Emery Gulash)*

NYC 77140 a 40' double door car from Lot 913B was at River Road in Reading, PA 2-25-70. The brown door on the Century green car was unfortunately all too typical of the Penn Central's attempts to keep everything out on the road without proper re-painting. Number 77000-77499 were built new in 1947-48 at DSI and converted from 760B at Beech Grove in 1962. *(C.T. Bossler)*

Fifty foot plug door box NYC 78965 was at So. Philadelphia 12-1-73. Lot 922B (78950-78999) were built at General American Company in December 1962. The cars had 2-piece movable bulkheads and 20'' cushion underframe for high class use in General Foods service. *(C.T. Bossler)*

Another 50' plug door car, NYC 48089 was at Reading, PA 6-6-71. Lot 931B (48000-48159) were built at DSI in 1964. The 4-belt "SL-2" cars had steel floors, doors, 20" cushion underframes, 70 ton trucks and 10' doors. *(C.T. Bossler)*

NYC 48222 was at Thorndale, PA 2-22-70. Lot 936B (48160-48259) consisted of 100 cars built at DSI in April 1964. Equipped with one-piece movable bulkheads and 6-position side wall fillers, the cargo was further protected by a cushion underframe with 20" travel. *(C.T. Bossler)*

Note the lack of black roof and ends on NYC 53179 at Rochester, NY in May 1964. The 60 foot double plug door car was part of Lot 938B (53179-53215 - 36 cars) built earlier that year at DSI. Assigned to Ford (Cleveland #1 plant) to carry 6-cylinder engines, it held 48 racks. Equipped with Keystone cushioning - 20" travel - it rode on 100 ton trucks. *(David McKay)*

Two views of a NYC classic: P&E 4503 at Peoria, Ill., January 7, 1961. Adorned with a *Quicker via Peoria* slogan riding a comet, the 50' single door car had an 8' door and load limit of 118,000 lbs. Lot 939B (4500-4544) consisted of 45 cars which were built a little more than a year earlier at DSI in 1959.   *(Sweetland collection)*

A less glamorous, all green P&E 4682 was at Dallas, Tex. on the MKT 7-3-66. Lot 944B (4600-4699 - 100 cars) was built at Pullman Standard in 1964. The 50' single door car had a load limit of 122,500 lbs. and light weight of 54,500 lbs. *(Dick Kuelbs)*

P&LE 6476 at an unknown location in September 1968 was a 50' plug door car from Lot 950B. This group (6450-6499) consisted of 50 cars built at DSI in 1964. With heavy duty wood floors, 9 SL-2 belt rails, cushion underframes with 20'' travel, 10'6'' doors, they rode on 70 ton trucks. *(collection of Dick Kuelbs)*

Another 50' plug door box, NYC 78798 was photographed at an unknown location in September 1970. Lot 953B (78750-78799 - 50 cars) was built at North American Car Co. in 1964. The RBL cars had a 10' door, load limit 139,800, lt. wt. 80200, 2-piece movable bulkheads, side wall fillers, and 20'' cushion underframe. They were used in Corn Products Company service. *(George Ford)*

An immaculately clean 50' single door was at Fort Worth, Texas in 1964. Lot 955B (6000-6449 - 450 cars) built at DSI in 1964-65 had adjustable belt rails, heavy duty wood floors, 10' doors and cushion underframes with 20'' travel.

(K.B. King Jr., Kuelbs collection)

Eighty-six foot long NYC 67210 was at Enola, PA 3-24-73. Lot 962B (67126-67280 - 155 cars) was constructed at Greenville Car Co. 4-65 and assigned to Ford service. With two movable bulkheads, 20'' cushioning, a 20' door, load limit 105,800, and lt. wt., 114200 the car exceeded Plate ''C'' dimensions.

(C.T. Bossler)

40' single door NYC 207270 was at Coatesville, PA 2-25-73. Lot 969B (207000-207499 - 500 cars) was a conversion project at Beech Grove in 1965. The 6' door (ld. limit 129100 lt wt 47900) cars were converted from Lot 743B cars (project 21).

(C.T. Bossler)

Big NYC 67363 was at Reading, PA 3-22-74. Lot 971B (67281-67381 - 101 cars) was built by Pullman-Standard 7-65. The 86' cars were assigned to Chrysler. With two large movable bulkheads, Pullman Hydro Frame cushioning (20'' travel), 20' door openings, inside ht. 12'9'', 70 ton trucks, and 33'' wheels, the car was classed XL according to the AAR.

(C.T. Bossler)

60' Double plug door NYC 53949 was in Texas in March 1968. Lot 987B (53860-53969) was built by Pullman-Standard in 1966. Its two 8' plug doors were used to load Ford bumpers at its Monroe, Mich. plant.

(Dick Kuelbs)

50' Double Door NYC 150595 was photographed in June 1969. Lot 992B (150550-150799 - 250 cars) was stretched from 40' double-door cars (Lots 760B & 913B - project 2) at Beech Grove Shops in 1967. Equipped with 50 ton trucks and 15'1¾'' door opening, they had a load limit of 116200 lbs and lightweight of 60,800 lbs.

(Dick Kuelbs collection)

▲ Double plug door NYC 67499 was at Thorndale, PA 4-25-72. Lot 993B (67382-67506 - 125 cars) was built at Greenville Car Co. 4-66. Assigned to Ford, they had cushioning with 20'' travel, 20' door opening, ld. lmt. 106,000, lt. wt. 113,600, 70-ton roller bearing trucks, two movable bulkheads and exceeded outside Plate ''C'' clearance.

(C.T. Bossler)

▼ Two very intriguing cars! NYC 92102 and 92101 were photographed at Mott Haven Yard, New York City 9-23-58. Lot 741B (cars 92100-92101 2 cars) were former C&O 19687 and 19749 built by ACF in 1957. Assigned to Flinkote Company service, they wore a unique blue paint with a never-seen-before NYC marking. Apparently an experiment that was not repeated, Century green box cars began coming out of the shops two months later.   *(R.S. Short)*

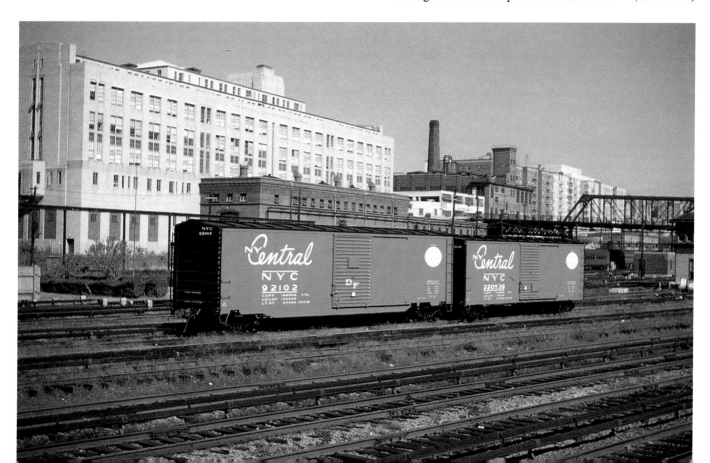

Outside-ribbed NYC 78599 was at Thorndale, PA 1-8-72. AAR designated "RBL" the 50' plug door cars had a capacity of 137,000 lbs. Lot 112B (78550-78699 - 150 cars) was built at DSI in 1966. *(C.T. Bossler)*

NYC 48285 from Lot 115B was at Dallas, Tex. on the SP in August 1976. The group 48260-48323 was built at DSI in 1966-67. With a capacity of 142,000 lbs, they had 10'6" plug doors. *(Ed Stoll)*

50' Plug Door NYC 48364 was at Dallas, Tex. in September 1976. Lot 132B (48360-48434) was a Pacific Car & Foundry Company order in 1967. With a 12'6" door opening, offset plug doors, capacity 142,600, 20" travel cushion underframe and movable bulkheads the car was used in can stock service. *(Ed Stoll)*

Very clean NYC 210067, a 50' single door car was at Syracuse, NY 10-3-67. Lot 135B (210000-210399 - 400 cars) had been just converted that same 1967 at Beech Grove shops from Lot 850B (Project 9).

(J.W. Swanberg)

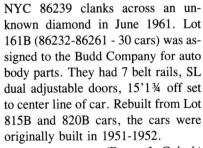

50' single door NYC 215147 was at Fleetwood, PA 3-15-70. Lot 136B (215000-215399 - 400 cars) was formerly 40' cars stretched to 50' at Beech Grove shops in 1967 (Project 8) from Lot 765B cars.

(C.T. Bossler)

NYC 86239 clanks across an unknown diamond in June 1961. Lot 161B (86232-86261 - 30 cars) was assigned to the Budd Company for auto body parts. They had 7 belt rails, SL dual adjustable doors, 15'1¾ off set to center line of car. Rebuilt from Lot 815B and 820B cars, the cars were originally built in 1951-1952.

(Emery J. Gulash)

Lot 147B NYC 69031 was at Detroit, MI 10-4-69. Nos. 69004-69129 were built by THRALL Co. in 1968 and assigned to Ford. This 86' cars had two movable bulkheads, cap. 152,000, Roller-Bearings and 100 ton trucks. *(J.W. Swanberg)*

NYC 67086 was photographed in a train at Northeast, PA in April 1968. Built by Pullman-Standard 2-65 it was assigned to auto parts service for Chevrolet. Lot 949B (67040-67096 - 57 cars) was a true "Hy - Cube" with capacity of 10,000 cu. ft. With Pullman Hydro Frame cushioning (20" travel), they had two 20' door openings per side to facilitate the loading/unloading of large auto parts.
(William F. Herrmann)

Built by Greenville in August 1966, a worn NYC 67540 was photographed at Third Street, Reading, PA on April 1, 1978. The Lot 103B car (67507-67552—46 cars) was assigned to Chrysler Corporation. The 86' long box car had a 20' door opening, 20" travel cushioning and two movable bulkheads. *(C.T. Bossler)*

Cabooses

▲ Waycar NYC 17836 was photographed at an unknown location in 1951. Built in 1895 as Michigan Central 2185, the 30' carbody had 5¼'' lap siding on its sides and ends. Such cars were rebuilt in 1925-29 with steel underframes. Painted oxide red, with safety yellow grab irons, its lettering was white in the seriff style without a NYC oval.

(J. Schmidt, Art Peterson collection)

▼ Another Michigan Central waycar, NYC 17841, was at Wayne, MI in January 1963. Built at Detroit in 1882 as MC Lot 191, when air brakes were installed, the cupola end became the A end, one window was removed and it was given a new paint job. Its tool box was located by the tross rods.

(Emery Gulash)

▲ NYC 17856 (former MC 2208) was at Ypsilanti, MI, in 1952. (Lot 367) (17850-17859—10 cars) was built at West Detroit in 1917-1920. The 32'6'' car shows its original painting arrangement with no logo. *(Emery Gulash)*

▼ NYC 17965 was built way back in 1886 and photographed 73 years later in September 1959. The car originally had 5 windows per side when it was built in St. Thomas shops in Canada in 1921 as Canadian Southern 23041. Note the black oval and white lettering.

(Emery Gulash)

NYC 17909 (the former MC 2267) was at Windsor, Ont station, June 1965. The 32½'' car was from Lot 471 constructed at West Detroit in 1924. It had 4 windows per side with the side cupola windows blanked out.
(Emery Gulash)

NYC 17919 was the former MC 2277 shown at Wayne, MI, Feb. 1967. Another Lot 471 waycar built at West Detroit in 1924, this example had cupola braces installed. It is seen on the Ford Truck Plant local coupled to SW-900 *8636 at the Wayne Freight House.   *(Emery Gulash)*

A side view of NYC 17906 (MC 2262) at Ypsilanti, MI, Jan. 1965. This Lot 429 32'6'' long car was built at West Detroit in 1921. It had four 20'' windows per side, 6'6'' between windows and was originally equipped with 5 oil lamps.   *(Emery Gulash)*

▲ Another distinctive, but different style of Central cabooses were the "Big Four" waycars. NYC 17560, former CCCS&L 445 was at Hubbard, OH, July 23, 1967. With a length of 32'0", height of 14'7¾", it was built at Beech Grove shop in 1912.   (Dave McKay)

▼ Big Four Caboose NYC 17577 (CCCS&L 473) was at Dewitt in 1963. Carrying the new NYC logo and new paint on its plywood sides, the three windows belie the fact that there were four originally. Three of its four journal box lids were up for oiling.   (Dennis Wood)

▲ Century green IHB 62 at McCook, IL 9/5/76 was a former AT&SF caboose. The all steel-riveted construction car had its cupola blanked off and the pseudo-Central IHB logo applied between windows. *(E. Roy Ward Collection)*

▼ IHB 275 was passing through Hammond, Ind, 6/62. IHB 275 and 276 were rebuilt from box cars during World War II. Originally painted red, the cars had a steel underframe, wooden body, and steel ends. In this photo its Century green body and unique yellow ends are apparent.
(Emery Gulash)

NYC 19026 was a NYC ''Standard'' waycar. Built in 1921 as part of Lot 427, the distinctive car was at Toledo 10-64 on a freight at the station.

(Emery Gulash)

Another NYC standard in new paint was NYC 19030 at Rochester, NY 10-61. Its length over end sills was 35'0'', height over rail 13'7/8'' with truck centers 20'0''. *(David McKay)*

NYC 19328, a wooden standard, was at Toledo in October 1964. The leaf springs on the ''T'' section caboose trucks are quite apparent.

(Emery Gulash)

Built in 1914, NYC standard 19194 was at Mott Haven 9-23-58. That day it was assigned to the local freight which had an RS3 for power.

(R.S. Short)

NYC Standard 19335 was built in 1887 and shown at Mott Haven Yard 12-1-66. Sporting a refurbished cupola, it wore the customary NYC oval logo.

(J.W. Swanberg)

NYC Standard 19450 works at Wayne, MI in December 1966. It and the NW-2 were on the local used to switch the Ford truck plant there.

(Emery Gulash)

▲ P&LE 160 rests at Budtown, PA in April 1968. The NYC standard waycar rode on T frame trucks.

(E. Roy Ward)

▼ Another NYC standard on the Pittsburgh & Lake Erie was P&LE 227 shown at Beaver Falls, PA in November 1968. It wore the black NYC oval above its P&LE reporting works. *(Emery Gulash)*

▲ A jazzed-up NYC standard was NYC 18096 at Toledo, OH 8-63. This was a safety campaign caboose—green with safety white stripe. Originally built in 1882, its sides have angle braces from body bolsters. *(Emery Gulash)*

▼ Another fancy NYC standard was P&E 21 at Avon Yard (Big Four Yard) in Indianapolis 8-63. It carried the *Quicker via Peoria* slogan and comet logo. *(Emery Gulash)*

NYC 18913 rests between local freight assignments at Indianapolis in August 1963. The wooden car was constructed almost fifty years earlier in 1914. *(Emery Gulash)*

NYC 18927 clatters across the diamonds at Vickers Jct. in Toledo, Ohio in 1953. The oval-less car carries red flags as its rear markers.

(Emery Gulash)

NYC 20144 was built at E. Buffalo during 1944 and photographed in April 1967. Lot 732 (20100-20149—50 cabooses) were 41' 4 5/8'' over strikers. Fifty wooden bodied box cars from Lots 234, 236, 240, and 262B were rebuilt into these cabooses. In 1946 five were painted into the *Pacemaker* color scheme—20112, 20117, 20129, 20132, and 20133.

(Emery Gulash)

▲ After World War II, the Central's first priority equipment-wise was to eliminate the steam locomotive in favor of the diesel. As we have seen in the previous two dozen photos, the road was still using hundreds of wood body cabooses built fifty to seventy years earlier and which were now overdue for replacement. It choose a cupola-less all-steel bay window design as the replacement. In June 1965, the old and new NYC waycars mingle at Toledo.

(Dwight Smith)

▼ The first of the new bay window waycars for the Central arrived in oxide red attire complete with NYC oval. This example hugs the rear of an eastbound through freight at Tower 66 crossing Woodbridge Avenue and Hoffman Street, Chatham, NY in 1956. *(George Ford)*

▲ Most fans remember the Central's bay window cars in the Century green attire. This is brand new NYC 21039 at Ann Arbor, MI in April 1963. Lot 919 (21000-21099) was built in 1963 by DSI. Painted with a Century green body with black roof and underframe, it carried a large 6'6'' x 3'1'' black, white and red NYC oval.   *(Emery Gulash)*

▼ A variation on the theme was NYC 20414 carrying a "Safety Wherever" admonition to stay alert. The white-striped car was passing through Dearborn, MI on a snowy day in January 1961. Part of Lot 827, it was one of the early bay window cars, built by St. Louis Car Company in 1952.   *(Emery Gulash)*

Unfortunately the Century green paint didn't hold up well and faded after a few years. This is NYC 21044 at Wyandotte, MI 3-66. It was built at DSI in 1963, part of Lot 919.

(Emery Gulash)

NYC 21511 at Dearborn with a faded *Road to the Future* slogan. Note the logo size and placement variation on the three bay window cabooses on this page.

(Emery Gulash)

P&LE 500 is at Newell PA in June 1970. Built by the P&LE in 1950, Lot 795 consisted of nos. 500-509.

(E. Ray Ward)

▲ A bright NYC 21574 carries a *Road to the Future* slogan on its sides at Youngstown, OH., 2-18-68. Part of Lot 827, it was built by St. Louis Car in 1952.   *(David McKay)*

▼ Large logo NYC 21719 was at Wyandotte, MI in March 1966. This car was also part of Lot 827 built at St. Louis Car Co. in 1952.   *(Emery Gulash)*

▲ Although the wooden cabooses were downgraded to use in yard, local and transfer service while the bay window cabooses took over the through freight assignments, by the mid-1960's the Central had found need of some modern waycars in transfer service. NYC 18060 is an example of the new transfer waycars built at DSI in 1966 as part of Lot 977 which was converted from Lot 703B.

(Emery Gulash)

▼ Another example is NYC 18087 shown in a B-end view at Detroit on July 23, 1966. The Lot 977 cars rode on Barber swing motion trucks. *(R.S. Short collection)*

Miscellaneous

▲ NYC 17746 carried a tank and pump for fueling diesels at a roundhouse. Shown at Lansing, Michigan in October 1958, this was the pump end of car (A end).

(Emery Gulash)

▼ NYC X1389 was an 8000 gallon tank mounted on a flat car. The combination tank/flat was at Elkhart, Indiana in May 1960.

(Emery Gulash)

P&LE X103001 was a non-revenue tank car photographed at McKees Rocks, PA 3-27-85. Such cars were used to transport diesel fuel to the P&LE McKees Rocks shops.

(E. Roy Ward)

NYC 16035 (Lot 831), was at Reading, PA, 1-25-73. The 12,000 gallon tank was built in 1952 and used in system diesel fuel service. The black car originally had a 28¼" x 19 1/8" NYC oval on the tank. Lot 831 (16000-16049) were 43'2" long, equipped with friction bearing trucks and built by Gen. American at Sharon, PA. *(C.T. Bossler)*

UTLX 20963 was the tank car seen coupled to X1389 on the opposite page at Elkhart, Ind., 5-60. The three dome tank car for fuel oil was on the siding for the Elkhart fuel station, along the mainline. This was a Central innovation to keep road freight power on its train on the mainline rather than uncoupling to run into the engine terminal. *(Emery Gulash)*

NYC X2921 was a 40' non-revenue flat at Harrisburg, PA, 6-10-72. This B-end view of the car shows the small crane for lifting bridge timbers on this Lot 255F car.   (C.T. Bossler)

NYC 36497 a non-revenue flat with sides was at Rutherford, PA 12-24-87. The Lot 598f, 42'1'' long car was built in January 1930 at Avis shops from group 496000-496299.

(H.E. Brouse)

NYC 29499 was a wheel car photographed at Reading, PA 4-23-77. Originally built by DSI in March 1941, it was rebuilt from a 52'7½'' flat from group 499100-499299. The Lot 690f car was used to move mounted wheels sets between the wheel shop and division car shops.

(C.T. Bossler)

P&LE X102008 a Lot 671H covered hopper was at McKees Rocks, PA 4-90. This company sand car held 1800 cubic feet of locomotive sand. They were coverted from 880500-880699 covered hoppers originally built by DSI in 1939. With 32'4 5/8'' in length over the strikers, they had 10 roof hatches per car with 3'x3' openings.
(Michael Bradley)

A NYC *Mercury* station wagon sits outside Ann Arbor Station 3-62. Equipped with hi-rail gear, it was used by the division superintendent. He was inside on the phone before he headed westbound on the NYC (MC) main. *(Emery Gulash)*

NYC Jeep #290 sits at Jackson, MI in 1951. The former US Army WWII Jeep was army surplus and used at the Jackson shops. *(Emery Gulash)*

▲ Wreck Derrick B&A X1653 was stationed at Weehawken, NJ when photographed in March 1961. The 100-ton Wrecking crane was formerly assigned to Worcester, MA. Built in 1907 by Industrial Works at Bay City, MI, it had a 26'3'' boom and was not self-propelled.   (Bob Hart)

▼ Detroit River Tunnel Co. #1 awaits a call at Livernois Yard, Detroit, in January 1960. The 100 ton crane had a special short boom for use inside its namesake tunnels to Canada.   (Emery Gulash)

▲ In a colorful period scene at Mott Haven Yard in the Bronx, the boom of crane X23 hangs over idler car X922 on September 23, 1958. The 120-ton crane was built by Industrial Works in 1913 as Lot 308W. The crane saw work in the Park Avenue approach tunnels to Grand Central Terminal, hence the angled boom.   *(R.S. Short)*

▼ Crane X27 wears the most up-to-date NYC "cigar band" look while at Detroit in February 1967. The all-black body of the 150-ton steam crane is relieved by safety yellow and red, while white canvas protects the cab from frigid winter winds.   *(Dick Kuelbs collection)*

NYC X90 was photographed at Jackson, MI in August 1963. Built by American, the diesel electric crane was used by the Central's Stores Department. *(Emery Gulash)*

NYC X62W and an all-Century green service train are backing down the main to clean a wreck at Harbor Creek, PA in May 1967. Seeing a headlight in the middle of a solid wall of flourescent tiger striping, it would be difficult to imagine what was approaching from a distance.

(William F. Herrman)

NYC X19531 was photographed at Detroit on May 1, 1965. The 150-ton steam wrecker was lifting a 10,000 gallon tank car by its dome batch.

(Emery Gulash)

▲ P&LE PS300505 is shown at Pittsburgh 3-2-74. The 150-ton diesel conversion was re-trucking a hopper near the P&LE station. Bored office workers across the Ohio River found this an interesting day to be looking out their windows. *(E. Roy Ward)*

▼ NYC X24 and X15 work together at Harbor Creek, PA in May 1967 to rerail a NYC Geep. X15 with a lifting bar on the Geep was using a light line; X24 with a coupler sling was using a heavy line. Lot 758 consisted of X13-X16 built by Industrial Works 1948-49.

(William F. Herman)

NYC X16693 a wreck train diner, at Harbor Creek, PA in May 1967. The Century green car was a wooden diner equipped with six-wheeled trucks and truss rods. *(William F. Herrmann)*

A NYC work train at the station in Westfield, NY, May 1967 is passed by GP7 #5674. The fully equipped work train has American Crawler cranes on the flat cars and maintenance-of-way material in the gons.
(William F. Herrmann)

NYC 8477, a wreck train work car was pictured at Youngstown, OH 5-4-68. The unique car was a cut-down combination baggage-coach.
(Dave McKay)

NYC X953 was another wreck train diner, photographed at Weehawken, NJ on the Central's River Line in March 1961. The classic old wood car was painted in the pre-Century green MofW scheme of red with a black roof. The six-wheeled car still had its truss rods. *(Bob Hart)*

Only a portion of X959 is visible out from under the bridge crossing at Mott Haven Yard on September 23, 1958. Apparently just repainted, the car served as a diner for MofW workers assigned to the wreck train.
(RS Short)

B&A X3707 was a "camp car" used in work train service when photographed on the Ware River Branch in Massachusetts, April 28, 1957. The 6-wheel trucked car formerly served as a coach hauling Boston commuters to work. *(William T. Clynes)*

A more utilitarian-looking camp car was NYC X22922 photographed in Michigan in 1946. Equipped with steel ends, wood sides and a center door, it had been converted from a box car. *(Emery Gulash)*

Very similar NYC X19069 was lensed seventeen years later at Ypsilante, MI in January 1963. The box car red cars had a minimum of identification or adornment, just a white stenciled reporting mark. *(Emery Gulash)*

Camp Car NYC X22483 is shoved at MP 34, east of Ann Arbor, Michigan in 1946. It served as the diner and lounge on this ballast train and was coupled to a MC style wooden caboose. *(Emery Gulash)*

▲ Camp Car NYC X15047 was photographed at Toledo, Ohio in 1946. Coverted from a wooden open platform coach, it had a kitchen on one end and a truss rod underframe.   *(Emery Gulash)*

▼ NYC X2148 was a tool car photographed in the light snow of Ann Arbor, Mich in March 1963. Converted from a wood RPO - Baggage car, it had 6-wheel trucks and a truss rod underframe.
(Emery Gulash)

▲ Another camp car was NYC X23367 photographed at Ann Arbor Station in September 1963. Somewhat more modern since it was converted from a steel coach, the all-silver car rode on 4-wheel trucks. *(Emery Gulash)*

▼ Having survived Penn Central and now two years into Conrail, a classic 1HB X252 rests in Chicago in December 1978. The wooded coach conversion is all jazzed up in Central Century green. *(William F. Herrmann)*

A twenty-two window coach now serves out its dotage as a "Rules Examination Car." The veteran was photographed at Albany Station in May 1966.

(Collectables from Bob's photos)

NYC X23500 was an Instruction car photographed at Syracuse, NY 10-3-67. Former coach #3118, it was used as an air brake training car and moved from division to division.

(J.W. Swanberg)

NYC X24192 was a work car when photographed on October 2, 1971. Converted from a WWII troop sleeper (end door), it had been used before on NYC as an express car.

(E. Roy Ward)

▲ Central "Safety car" X23177 was lensed by official photographer Ed Nowak at the West Albany, NY shops. Inside employees were given safety lectures and shown a short movie on how to avoid injury in the dangerous world of railroading.*(Ed Nowak, Morning Sun Books Collection)*

▼ NYC X26138 photographed at Collinwood Yard outside Cleveland, Ohio on February 23, 1967 once rode behind a mighty L-2 4-8-2 Mohawk. It was now used as a "diesel fuel car." *(Dave McKay)*

NYC X1413 a Flanger was photographed at Corning, NY 5-17-64. Equipped with two cupolas for ease of operation in both directions, it had a steel underframe and wooden body. The two flanger blades for operation in either direction were in the center of car. *(David R. Connor)*

Flanger NYC X705 was at Peekskill, NY in March 1962. This was a one-cupola flanger with steel ends with a door at the end and a side door at center. The flanger blade was just behind the trucks.

(Matthew J. Herson, Jr., Kuelbs collection)

NYC X773 was the special electrified territory flanger photographed at Harmon, NY on June 12, 1967. Built by Wendell & McDuffie Company in 1927, the Lot 2057 car had an extra long cupola and steam jets connected via a steam line to an accompanying electric locomotive. The steam jets and third rail shoes helped clear the electric system of snow and ice.

(J.W. Swanberg)

▲ NYC X6316M was at Livernois Yard in Detroit in May 1967. Built by Jordan Spreader in E. Chicago, the Model J had an all black body, yellow safety appliances, and silver plow stripes, with operating wings on both sides. It was part of Lot 750 (11 spreader Ditchers) built in 1945-46.

(Emery Gulash)

▼ Boston & Albany X1435 was photographed at Palmer, Mass. on October 9, 1954. This was a two-cupola flanger designed for the best view possible regardless of the direction used.

(William T. Clyner)

▲ Snow Plow NYC X663 was in the midst of Central snow territory at Erie, Pa in March 1966. This unit was a single track plow built by Russell in 1941. Now in all-red paint, the Lot 705 plow was originally intended for use in Watertown, NY. *(William F. Hermann)*

▼ NYC X665 was at Livernois Yard, Detroit, 5-67. The Russell Snow Plow Company built this plow at Ridgeway, PA in 1944. Now attired in 3 colors, the Lot 727 single track plow had doors under the plow to oil journal boxes. *(Emery Gulash)*

▲ NYC X27208, a Jet Snow Blower, was at Delray, MI 3-68. Built from cut-down caboose #18002, it was used to melt away snow accumulation in the tracks and switches. Constructed at Collinwood shops in 1963, it used a G.E. J-47 jet engine modified to burn diesel fuel supplied by a tank car. *(Emery Gulash)*

▼ The X27208 in operation at Hamtramek, MI 3-6-65. Here it is in service clearing switches for the support yard at the "Home of Plymouth Autos" being pushed along by an RS-11. *(J.D. Hediger, Emery Gulash collection)*

▲ Always known for its innovation, another Central jet snow blower was NYC DS1-20 at East Rochester, NY 1-20-67. Built at DSI East Rochester Shops, it had one support fuel tank and a natty Century green safety stripe paint job. *(J.W. Swanberg)*

▼ NYC X29493, another Jet snow blower, was at Delray, MI in October 1965. Built on a 52' flat car, it had eight support fuel tanks. *(Emery Gulash)*

▲ NYC XH-8, steam heat trailer, was at Poughkeepsie, NY 8-25-68. Its general steel casting trucks with 5½x10 journals, carried the steel car body which was 35'6½ long over coupler pulling faces. The car had two water tanks with total capacity of 1342 tons and an oil tank of 204 gallons. *(R.S. Short)*

▼ NYC XH-8 again, this time at Harmon, NY and six years later on 8-6-74. Lot 2124 consisted of eight steam heat trailers built at Harmon in 1931 and 1932. They were used behind non-boiler equipped electric "motors." Their underframes came from K-3 steam locomotive tenders. H-1 was built 10-31, last one (H-8) in April 1932. The H-8 was later equipped with a 4625 vapor steam generator. *(J.W. Swanberg)*

▲ The Central had a fleet of trucks used to take L.C.L. (less than car load) shipments from rail heads to non-rail served customers. This service peaked with *Pacemaker* LCL service which was exemplified here in this November 16, 1949 scene at Indianapolis, Indiana. The grey-bodied single-axle van has been loaded with cargo from the F3-powered *Pacemaker* box car train.

(Ed Nowak, Morning Sun Books collection)

▼ Seeking ways to reduce its long haul passenger losses in the 1950's, the Central made several stabs at using lightweight equipment. Besides the General Motors *Aerotrain*, the road tried out *Train X, The Xplorer*. The Pullman-Standard-built cars show their yellow window stripe to advantage in this Ed Nowak photo. The train was pulled by a unique Baldwin-Lima-Hamilton cab unit.

(Ed Nowak, Morning Sun Books collection)

▲ The NYC Beech Grove Shops is pictured in August 1963 with a 50' double door box car out front. The car was from Lot 692-B (176200-176799) built in DSI in 1941.
(Emery Gulash)

▼ Another view of the NYC Beech Grove Shops that same day. The building was constructed in 1907 as the shops for the Big Four System.
(Emery Gulash)

▲ At the NYC Despatch Shops in East Rochester, NY in February 1967, a production run of P&LE gons in primer paint is apparent. The Lot 871-G 52'-6'' gons (P&LE 13000-13999) were early all-welded cars, and had many production and quality control problems. *(J.W. Swanberg)*

▼ The NYC Freight House at Ann Arbor, Mich 3-61. Just a nice selection of NYC box cars, a NYC Freight house, MofW employees with lunch pails and truck, and a 10-ton electric crane on the team track. *(Emery Gulash)*

Two of our favorite NYC heralds close out our tribute to New York Central equipment. *(Above)* the ''modern'' or ''cigar band'' Central logo on a Century green background (Lot 742B) painted in July 1959 and *(below)* the erstwhile *Early Bird* logo from a 1957 Lot 862B box.

(Top - Emery Gulash, bottom - E. Ray Ward)

Occasional Paper 56

Early Vitreous Materials

Edited by
M. Bimson and I. C. Freestone

Department of Scientific Research 1992

BRITISH MUSEUM OCCASIONAL PAPERS

Publisher :   British Museum
                         Great Russell Street
                         London WC1B 3DG

Production Editor: Denny Hemming

Distributor :   British Museum Press
                         46 Bloomsbury Street,
                         London WC1B 3QQ

Occasional Paper No. 56, 1992:

Early Vitreous Materials
M. Bimson and I.C. Freestone

First published in 1987

© Trustees of the British Museum

ISBN 0 86159 056 2

ISSN 0142 4815

Orders should be sent to British Museum Press.
Cheques and postal orders should be made payable to
British Museum Press and sent to 46 Bloomsbury
Street, London WC1B 3QQ. Access, American Express,
Barclaycard and Visa credit cards are accepted.

Printed and bound by the British Museum
Reprographic Unit.